ETERNAL
DESERT

DAVID MUENCH

FRANK WATERS

AN ARIZONA HIGHWAYS BOOK

To
*the inheritors
of the earth—*
Our
children

(LEFT) SANTA RITA MOUNTAINS, ARIZONA.
(COVER ONLAY AND TITLE PAGE) DESERT STORM,
SAGUARO NATIONAL MONUMENT, ARIZONA.

ETERNAL DESERT

PHOTOGRAPHY BY DAVID MUENCH
TEXT BY FRANK WATERS
TEXT EDITING, BERNARD L. FONTANA
VISUAL EDITING AND DESIGN, GARY M. AVEY

Editor's note:

The italicized passages which appear with the photographs in this book are excerpted from the second edition of *The Desert*, by John C. Van Dyke (1856-1932), originally published in 1903. While Van Dyke's book is known to a handful of desert lovers, his words have by no means reached the audience they deserve. He was genuinely the pioneer of desert appreciation in North America.

In re-reading *The Desert*, I soon realized that we have something close to a perfect fit between David Muench's photographs and Van Dyke's words. It is almost as if Muench carried a copy of Van Dyke with him when he took his pictures. Moreover, Van Dyke's words beautifully complement those of Frank Waters, underscoring many of the points—and the views—which Frank expresses in his own prose.

— Bernard L. Fontana

THE ETERNAL DESERT
Prepared by the Related Products Section of *Arizona Highways* magazine, a publication of the Arizona Department of Transportation.

Hugh Harelson—Publisher/ Wesley Holden—Managing Editor/ Robert J. Farrell—Associate Editor. Pat Kenny Graphic Design— Production. Copyright ©1990 by the Arizona Department of Transportation, State of Arizona. All rights reserved. No part of this book may be reproduced in any form or means without permission from *Arizona Highways*, 2039 West Lewis Avenue, Phoenix, AZ 85009.

Library of Congress Catalog Number
89-83442
ISBN 0-916179-22-2
Printed in Japan

(OPPOSITE) STAINED SANDSTONE, PARIA CANYON, PARIA CANYON-VERMILION CLIFFS WILDERNESS, ARIZONA-UTAH. (INSET) YUCCAS, WHITE SANDS NATIONAL MONUMENT, NEW MEXICO.

TABLE OF CONTENTS

(OPPOSITE) DESERT PAVEMENT, SONORAN DESERT, ARIZONA.
(INSET) SAGUARO SUNSET.

There is no sunlight
(in "Sunny Italy" or in the
"clear light of Egypt")
compared with that which
falls upon the upper reaches
of the Sierra Madre or the
uninhabitable wastes of the
Colorado Desert.

SUNSET, SUPERSTITION MOUNTAINS,
SUPERSTITION WILDERNESS,
ARIZONA.

*W*ho shall paint the
splendor of (the desert's) light;
and from the rising up of
the sun to the going down of
the moon over the iron
mountains, the glory of its
wondrous coloring!

VERMILION CLIFFS
AND ERODED REMNANTS OF DUNES
IN NAVAJO SANDSTONE
IN THE VERMILION CLIFFS-
PARIA CANYON WILDERNESS,
ARIZONA-UTAH.

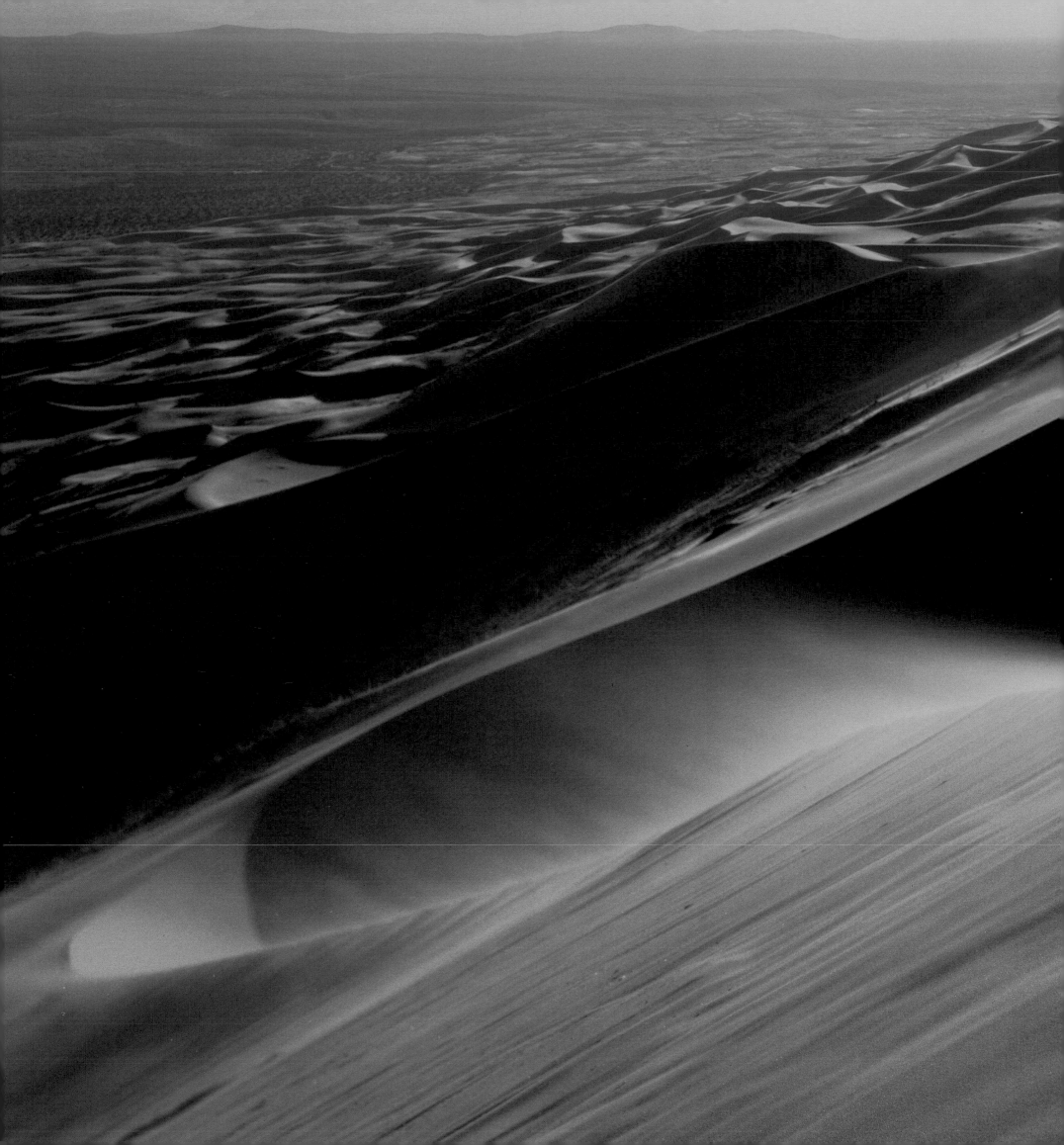

The shifting sands! Slowly they move, wave upon wave, drift upon drift; but by day and by night they gather, gather, gather. They overwhelm, they bury, they destroy, and then a spirit of restlessness seizes them and they move off elsewhere, swirl upon swirl, line upon line, in serpentine windings that enfold some new growth or fill in some new valley in the waste.

KELSO DUNES,
MOJAVE DESERT,
CALIFORNIA.

The voiceless river!
From the canyon to the sea
it flows through deserts,
and ever the seal of silence
is upon it.

GILA RIVER, ARIZONA.

15

Hardiest of the hardy
are these plants
and just as fierce
in their ways as
the wild cat.
You cannot touch
them for the claw.

OCOTILLO AND SAGUARO
IN THE SONORAN DESERT,
TOHONO O'ODHAM INDIAN
RESERVATION, ARIZONA.

17

Of a simple nature,
(the Indians) have lived
in a simple way,
close to their Mother Earth
beside the desert they loved,
and (let us believe it!)
nearer to the God
they worshipped.

BETATAKIN RUIN "HILLSIDE HOUSE",
OCCUPIED BETWEEN 1242 AND 1300,
NAVAJO NATIONAL MONUMENT, ARIZONA.

THE ETERNAL DESERT

Not long ago, when measured by the sands of the eternal desert, early American settlers venturing westward regarded almost the entire western United States as the "Great American Desert." Its vast wilderness was known to contain some high snowy peaks, ranges of forested mountains, and watered valleys, but verified tales of travelers perishing of thirst in its baking sandy wastes pictured the desert best.

If the Great American Desert was then largely imaginative, later familiarity with it established under the name of the North American Desert the actual existence of a long arid region stretching 2,300 miles southward from the state of Washington into northern Mexico, including the peninsula of Baja California. Covering 500,000 square miles, this great desert ranks fifth in size among the deserts in the world. Its combined area comprises one-seventh of the land surface of our global earth, and it possesses the same general characteristics everywhere.

It has often struck me how comparable is the desert in our outer world and the realm of the unconscious in our inner world. Each is the substratum of the living being in which it is embodied.

The earth's desert and man's unconscious have been partially explored and tentatively defined, but not fully understood. Constantly expanding and shrinking, jutting out unexpectedly into areas under domestic control, their functional domains never remain the same. Both serve as repositories of mankind's long past. Excavated from the ever-shifting desert sands are crude stone tools and ancient monuments, fallen temples once erected to unknown gods, even the ruins of buried cities. So, too, from the unconscious are exhumed vestigial memories of our earliest instincts and desires. The changing aspects of each evoke equally the terror of an impersonal cruelty and the peace of healing silence, and so seem mysteriously impervious to the flow of time.

This aura of the eternal unknown always has distinguished the desert from other landscapes on the variegated surface of our earth. It is a great mesmerizer, reflecting all the shapes of our imagination. So it was with me. Mountain-born in the Colorado Rockies, I had not seen the desert until as a young traffic engineer I was sent by the telephone company into the desert embracing the Salton Sink and the Imperial Valley, near the Mexican border in California. From there I made a long horseback trip through Baja California. The appalling immensity and emptiness of the desolate region seemed at once repellent and alluring. How stark and strange it spread around me! Tawny, bare rock mountains rearing from their *bajadas* of tumbled boulders. Valley floors shimmering in the pitiless glare of the sun and reflected heat waves. Shadows of clouds drifting over *playas* of white alkali. Fantastic skeletal shapes of spiny trees outlined against the horizon. A world of mystical unreality beyond the comprehension of the eye and mind. And over all a subtle lilac-tinted haze. Time, I felt, completed its circle here. Was this how the green world I had known began, or did the desert project its eventual end?

The fascination impelled by the desert can't be explained even by those who have experienced it. Even now, so many years later when my wife and I live much of the year on the desert west of Tucson, Arizona, it still sometimes evokes from my unconscious odd dreams of fragmented residual images as of our aeonian lifespan.

The North American Desert is divided into four distinctive segments. The Great Basin Desert on the north covers parts of Oregon with a spur into Washington, most of Nevada and Utah, and portions of Wyoming, Colorado, Arizona, and California. The Mojave Desert below it lies in southeastern California, southern Nevada, and northwestern Arizona. Extending south, the Sonoran Desert spreads over southern California, southern Arizona, and Mexico's State of Sonora, and the Baja California peninsula.

Another large segment, the Chihuahuan Desert, embraces some of southeastern Arizona, part of southern New Mexico, and a southwestern portion of Texas, continuing down through Chihuahua, Coahuila, and other states in Mexico.

These regional areas, interlocked segments of the whole, have their own physical characteristics which largely determine the living forms within them. All are dry and hot enough to meet the rule-of-thumb definition of a desert as a region having an annual rainfall of 10 inches or less and high temperatures.

In shape the North American Desert is an irregular elongated trough whose lowest spots are Death Valley in the Mojave Desert, 282 feet below sea level, and Salton Sink in the Sonoran Desert, 235 feet below sea level. The average annual rainfall in Death Valley is 1.63 inches, and it holds the high temperature record for the Western Hemisphere, 134 degrees F. (the world record of 136.4 degrees being recorded at El Azizia, Libya.) Measurements in the Salton Sink and in the giant sand dunes of the Gran Desierto of Mexico lie within a comparable range.

Since temperature drops 2.5 degrees for every 1,000 feet rise in altitude, and the North American Desert gradually rises from south to north, the driest and hottest region in general is the southern and lowest part of the Sonoran Desert. This bears out the report of Peggy Larson in *The Deserts of the Southwest* that the lowest annual rainfall of 1.2 inches has been measured at Bataques, Mexico.

Aside from these dry-and-hot statistics, we can perhaps view best the desert as an eternal component of our global earth by observing its relationship with those anciently recognized four primary elements — water, air, earth, and fire. The ancient Greeks believed they are the constituents of our own human bodies. From them are born all other mineral, plant, and animal forms, and they largely shape the physical features and changing moods of the desert. ☐

WATER

Water comprises nearly three-fourths of the body of man and the surface of our planet. No one questions its importance, but few persons associate the "waterless desert" with water. Yet the desert always contains water. Without water its many plant and animal life forms could not exist. And some of the first chapters in the desert's biography have been written by water.

During the Pleistocene Era, 75,000 to 10,000 years ago by geological reckoning, glaciers inched down into the great basin between the Sierra Nevada and Cascade mountains on the west and the Rockies on the east. About 15,000 years ago they began to melt and retreat, leaving innumerable lakes. The largest was Lake Bonneville, 1083 feet deep, covering 20,000 square miles in Utah and Nevada. The Great Basin Desert today preserves the memory of the ancient inland sea in the present Great Salt Lake, which covers about 2,000 square miles, and is flanked by the barren Bonneville Salt Flats. Still fed by drainage from the surrounding mountains, and having no outlet, the lake's salt content is about eight times greater than that of the ocean. So salty is the water that a swimmer in it cannot sink.

The desert's preservation of its watery past is also found in Salton Sink, located in the southern California portion of the Sonoran Desert. Its below-sea-level depression was once inundated by the Gulf of California. Gradually the Colorado River, flowing to the east of the Sink and swollen with silt gorged out of Grand Canyon, built up a delta across the mouth of the gulf creating ancient Lake Cahuilla which evaporated at the annual rate of more than a hundred feet. Whether it finally dried up or still existed in historic time is not known, although Cocopah and Cahuilla Indian legends preserve memories of it. And from the old dirt road passing Travertine Rock and Coral Reef you can see the ancient

*The desert rainfall comes
quickly and goes quickly.
...There's none of it
remains upon the surface
except perhaps ... a catch of water
in a rocky bowl
of some canyon.*

TINAJAS ALTAS,
AT THE EDGE OF THE LECHUGUILLA DESERT, NEAR THE
CABEZA PRIETA NATIONAL WILDLIFE REFUGE, ARIZONA.

southwestern New Mexico, it flows southwesterly to its confluence with the Colorado. A desert river after leaving New Mexico, the Gila is alternately a wide sandy arroyo and a raging muddy torrent. Yet its banks have been inhabited by the prehistoric Mogollon and Hohokam, and by historic Apaches, Pimas, Maricopas, and Tohono O'odham.

David F. Costello in *The Desert World* reminds us that water is the only mineral that exists in solid, liquid, or gaseous state. As a gas it affects humidity, condensing to form dew. As a solid it forms ice which fractures rocks and cracks the thin layer of soil in the mountains. And in liquid state it creates not only lakes and rivers, but special features in desert landscapes.

The *playa*, a Spanish word meaning a "beach," is one such feature. It is a flat lake bed whose rainwater has evaporated, leaving its leached alkali to be baked by the sun into a dazzling white, smooth floor resembling a seaside beach. Sunrises and sunsets turn the surface of such playas yellow, orange, and red. *Tinajas* or tanks are found in the parched desert hills along the rugged Camino del Diablo which parallels the Arizona-Sonora border between Sonoyta and Yuma. They are small rock basins or potholes which retain water from infrequent rains. Providing the only water to birds and other animals for miles around, they have saved the lives of former Indian inhabitants, prospectors, immigrants, adventurers, and other desert travelers.

Alluvial fans spread out from the base of nearly every desert range. Consisting of rock and gravel washed down the clefts in the steep walls, they appear from a distance like graceful fans opened to waft away the cloying heat. *Bajadas* or "slopes" are more shapeless. Great declines of boulders and rock slides may extend for miles as do lava badlands known as *malpais*. Such Spanish names aptly described the features of the Sonoran Desert first seen by *conquistadores* centuries ago, and are still generally used everywhere.

beach line marking high water like a ring around a bath tub.

Formation of the present Salton Sea is comparatively recent. In 1901 the California Development Company began the ambitious project of diverting water from the Colorado River into what was still known, when I lived there, as the Colorado Desert. The river was tapped near Yuma, Arizona, channeled west through the border region of Baja California, then diverted north into the lower Salton Sink. With irrigation the barren wasteland blossomed. It produced six cuttings of alfalfa a year, long-staple cotton yielding more than a bale to the acre, and, maturing in May, the first melons to reach breakfast tables in Chicago and New York. The desolate desert took on the regal name of Imperial Valley, the "Winter Garden of America." Farmers and ranchers flocked in. Towns were established. But in August, 1905, disaster struck. Swollen by flood, the always rambunctious Colorado River tore through its channels and burst into Imperial Valley, pouring as much as 90,000 cubic feet of water per second into Salton Sink. Before the flow was finally stopped in February, 1907, it had submerged the New Liverpool Salt Company works under 60 feet of water and created the present Salton Sea, 235 feet below sea level. It is now 45 miles long, 17 miles wide, and 83 feet deep, a salty reminder of ancient Lake Cahuilla.

Two principal rivers course through the Sonoran Desert. In addition to the mighty Colorado on the west, the broad Gila River, with its Salt River tributary, sweeps through and drains much of southern Arizona. Rising in the mountains of

Rainfalls on the desert are sudden, few, and far apart. Most of them last only a few minutes and are known as *temporales*. Even so, they cause flash floods which quickly fill dry washes and sandy arroyos. Rule number one for campers is never to spread their blankets and gear for the night in such wind-protected, soft depressions however clear the sky.

The curious affinity and opposition between the desert and water are dramatically visible during a storm when slanting sheets of silver rain descend from the sky but never reach the earth. But cloudbursts do occur. Standing in an open *abra*, or valley, within the outstretched paws of a rocky sierra, you can watch the black-humped clouds herding together overhead. A flash of vivid blue lightning, quick as the strike of a serpent, is followed by a sharp rattle and an ominous roar echoed by the desert mountains. Then comes the rain with all the fury of a force pent up for months then suddenly released. Wide river beds, dry for years, swell into raging torrents. Stout bridges crumble like match sticks. Blocks of asphalt paving are swept away like chips of bark. Telephone lines disappear. Then, its fury spent, the storm is over, having demonstrated the power of water to alter even slightly the face of the eternal desert. □

FIRE

Father Sun, of course, is the ultimate source of heat and life for Mother Earth; the blazing symbol of the element fire. The desert, of all land surfaces, is its chief recipient and reflector.

As there is little cloud cover and almost no moisture in the air, the desert receives about 90 percent of the sun's radiation. This accounts for its high temperatures, like the 134 degrees recorded at Death Valley. Little wonder that the Shoshonean Indians called Death Valley "Ground on Fire" and the region northeast of Las Vegas "Valley of Fire."

There are many other notable hot spots. Yuma has recorded 123 degrees, and its days receive 93 percent sunshine yearly. I remember the sign above the door of the lunchroom at the old railroad station years ago: "Free Meals Every Day the Sun Doesn't Shine."

Years of constant exposure to the searing rays of the sun creates, on the surface of rocks on the desert and in mountain foothills, a curious shiny glaze known as "desert varnish." It is believed to be the result of deposits of microbes that utilize manganese and iron in the atmosphere's dust for energy.

Discoloration of exposed glass is more familiar. When my sister lived in Sedona, Arizona, she often spent Sunday afternoons prodding in the dump below the nearby mining town of Jerome, picking up long discarded whiskey flasks. The main objects of her search were occasional small opium bottles once owned by Chinese workers in the mines. All the bottles and flasks had changed color to a delicate lilac, almost the same tint as the faint desert haze. Such bottles are prized by collectors.

Desert travelers who don't take precautions may suffer heat exhaustion, dehydration, and even death.

Curiously enough, the desert's extreme daytime heat is matched by its nighttime cold. Most of the surface heat is radiated back into the sky after sundown, which can result in a drop of temperature to below freezing in winter. My brother-in-law and I once experienced this when we camped at Dante's View overlooking Death Valley. We had driven the long way into the Valley from the old mining towns of Randsburg and Johannesburg in the Mojave Desert, and over Wingate Pass, through a horror of sharp volcanic rock, and, following faint wheel tracks, through dry washes. It was dark when we arrived at the overlook and we were dead tired. Small branches and twigs of brush supplied the only wood for a fire which burned out faster than we could gather more. We soon gave up the effort and crawled between our

The dunes are always rhythmical and flowing in their forms; and for color, the desert has nothing that surpasses them.

CADIZ VALLEY DUNES, MOJAVE DESERT, CALIFORNIA.

blankets. It became impossible to continue lying down. The ground exuded cold as if it were a chunk of ice, penetrating to our very bones. I think I've never been as cold in my life.

We huddled there, staring down into that long serpentine Valley narrowly constricted between the walls of the Grapevine and Funeral mountains on the east, and the Panamints on the west. Eerily beautiful in moonlight, it looked like something a man might someday glimpse on the surface of a yet unvisited moon. Its deceptively smooth floor of alkali flats, deposits of borax, sodium, magnesium, and other minerals washed down from the mountains, gleaming incandescent white by day, now shone faintly blue. And upon this ghostly moonscape were cast the purple shadows of the mountains. Then suddenly, with sunrise, it all became a blinding white; an ample reward for our trip. □

AIR

The element air, our atmosphere, is an upper sea surrounding our planet and extending 50 miles above its surface. About 15 miles up it contains a thin layer of ozone, a special form of oxygen which absorbs ultraviolet light rays from the sun. Without this protective shield we would be exposed to the full power of these dangerous rays.

This atmospheric sea, or envelope, is in constant motion. It circulates throughout the world in orderly movements like the great currents of the watery sea. Air ascends over warm areas and descends upon cool areas, following the day and night and seasonal changes of temperatures—the "breathing of the continents."

The desert in general is a high pressure area in which cool air becomes warmer and holds moisture instead of releasing it. Mountains also help to alter the air currents.

The Great Basin Desert is flanked by high ranges on the east and west, and within it rise many parallel north-south ranges. The prevailing air flow from the Pacific Ocean rises on the windward side of the Cascade and Sierra Nevada ranges. The moist air becomes cool, and releases heavy falls of rain and snow. As it crosses to the leeward side of the mountains, the air becomes warmer, decreasing precipitation, and leaving the land dry. The aridity of the Chihuahuan Desert, lying between two high ranges, is partly caused by the same pattern. A different condition exists in the coastal Baja California region of the Sonoran Desert. The chill air from the cool Pacific Ocean currents holds only enough moisture to condense into fog. Little rain falls because the air above the desert is warm and prevents precipitation. This creates a unique coastal desert atmosphere.

Air is not restricted to moving in ordered flows. It too, like water, sun-fire, and earth, is a living element that seems to possess a willful and capricious nature of its own. It reveals quirks of mood and unpredictable changes of direction. Little currents like wayward children scamper anywhere, anytime.

On a hot summer day as you are standing on a high ridge and looking out at the flat open desert, you will likely see a tall serpent-like figure suddenly rise out of the unbroken sand. Gyrating like a whirling dervish, and gliding majestically and smoothly across the valley floor, it resembles one of those mysterious, tall, godlike figures anciently depicted on cliff walls. These whirling serpentine figures are known as dust devils and are superstitiously believed to be lost souls or malevolent spirits of the dead. Whirlwinds of dust, they may rear hundreds of feet high. Just as suddenly, they disappear.

Sandstorms are not so entrancing. The aerial sea is

sometimes aroused to a fury of high winds that whip up brownish clouds of dust and sand which blot out the sun and may last for days.

Wind is an inalienable part of the desert everywhere. For some reason I always think of the Mojave as a perpetual wind-blown expanse under a brassy sky. I can understand better why the wind blows constantly through San Gorgonio Pass just above the Salton Sink. It is one of the greatest drafts known. From the desert below, the rising hot dry air tends to create a vacuum toward which rushes the cool moist air from the Pacific coast. Stopped by the high San Bernardino and San Jacinto mountains, its only inlet is the pass, so through it blows a constant wind.

Abrasive sand-laden air carves from rock outcrops a fantastic assortment of needlepoint spires, ungainly buttes, and balanced rocks. It also creates dynamic sand dunes. Small seas of sand without a leaf of green, their soft shimmering waves seem to roll and slowly break against the horizon. The White Sands near Alamogordo, New Mexico, are probably the most dazzling dunes in the world. They consist of pure white gypsum, reflecting the blinding glare of the noonday sun, changing to warmer-hued colors at sunrise and sunset and cool colors in moonlight.

Less spectacular but as well-known to travelers are the yellow Algodones Sand Dunes near Yuma, Arizona. Covering an area 50 miles by five miles they historically presented the typical image of the "Great American Desert" envisioned a century ago—a sea of shifting billows of sand in which a voyager would be lost if he attempted to cross it.

The dunes still presented problems, often humorous, after a plank road had been laid across them in 1916. I still remember it. A roller-coaster of a road, it climbed to the crest of one dune, then plunged down into a trough before climbing to the next. Often called the Corduroy Road, it was made of railroad ties laid crosswise, and was just wide enough for one auto to drive upon. At infrequent intervals a short spur to one side was provided so a car could turn off and wait for an approaching car to pass. This posed a traffic problem even then, as two approaching cars often met between widely separated turnoffs, and one of them would be required to back up on the narrow plank road. Which one was the question that usually resulted in profane arguments, giving rise to the name of "goddamns" for these turnoffs.

Dunes, wherever they are, demonstrate in slow motion a curious similarity to the sea. Forever shifting under the constant wind, one grain of sand at a time sliding down from the crest of a wave into the trough below, dunes show the ability of the desert to accommodate changes without changing.

Mirages, of course, may be the supreme phenomena achieved in the desert by the element air. In the distance you see an enticing lake which turns out when you reach it to be only an expanse of sand. Atmospheric physics professors explain that the phenomenon occurs just above a warm surface when the temperature has decreased with height and the curvature of the sun's rays is greatest. Often an object above ground level appears to be below the surface and is inverted. Rather than slaking our thirst with these optical explanations, it is easier to accept the fact that air, earth, and sun have collaborated magically to contrive the illusionary presence of the absent fourth element, water. □

EARTH

The desert is a part of the upper mantle of our planet's surface which gives birth to all living forms. The desert supports a cover of sparse vegetation uniquely adapted to it.

Each of the four segments of the North American Desert nourishes a predominant form of plant life. That of the Great Basin Desert is the big sagebrush *(Artemisia tri-*

dentata), a gray-green bush or shrub with three wedge-shaped leaves, which grows up to seven feet high. There are many species—black, red, and the color of Zane Grey's popular Western novel *Riders of the Purple Sage.* Sage or sagebrush is one of the more prevalent shrubs throughout the entire West and one of the more useful. Its leaves, seeds, and bark supply food to birds, rodents, and grazing animals. The leaves, boiled in water, make a bitter tea that mothers of past generations made children drink to cure bilious spells. Today, like my Indian friends, I pluck a leafy branch, crunch it in my palms, and wipe my cheeks with its wild sweet smell. As incense it perfumes the house when you light a branch from the fireplace and carry it through the rooms.

The Joshua tree *(Yucca brevifolia)* is always associated with the windswept Mojave Desert; it grows naturally nowhere else. Weirdly outlined against the sky, the giant-size yucca rears 20 or more feet high. Trunk and branches bristle with spines and sawtooth stilettos. Joshua trees live as long as a century.

Prominent in many areas of the Sonoran and Chihuahuan deserts are various species of agave, widely known as the century plant. One of these, *Agave lechuguilla,* is the trademark of the Chihuahuan Desert. It is a low plant spreading out a rosette of waxy sharp-pointed leaves two or three feet long. From the center the *lechuguilla* at maturity sprouts a bare 10-foot stalk bearing glossy yellow blossoms that are often tinged with red or purple. They seem to light up the stark brown hillsides, and it is little wonder they bear the Spanish name of *Las Velas del Cristo,* "Candles of the Lord."

Our popular name "century plant" stems from the belief that the blossoming stalk appears only once in a hundred years. Actually, agaves bloom at widely varying times depending on the species and environmental circumstances, and none lives a hundred years. After the plant blooms it dies.

Agaves are easily confused with yuccas. Each puts up a bare stalk flowering with blossoms. The yucca, however, has a thick trunk growing shoulder high, whereas agaves grow close to the ground. And unlike agaves, yuccas don't die after blossoming.

Several species of agave, called "maguey," have been used throughout Mesoamerica for thousands of years. Parts of their fleshy, succulent leaves are still roasted in pits for food. Their sugary sap furnishes a non-alcoholic drink, *aguamiel,* and, in fermented form, a beer call *pulque.* Spaniards introduced the technique of distillation, and two more agave drinks, both potent in alcoholic content, have been the result: mescal and tequila.

The squashed leaves of *Agave schottii,* commonly known as "amole," provide soap for washing hair and clothes. The fibers of *lechuguilla* are commercially woven into twine, rope, mats, rugs, and curtains. And in Arizona, experiments are being made to grow agaves as a major crop.

The popular symbol of the Sonoran Desert is the saguaro cactus *(Cereus giganteus).* Address it please, if you will, as "Grandfather," the Indian term acknowledging respect for one's age and accomplishments. The favorite homeland of this giant cactus is the desert around Tucson, Arizona. One of the saguaro elders, 52 feet high, was rooted here on land that then belonged to Mexico, long before the signing of the Declaration of Independence.

The saguaro's massive green trunk is fluted and covered with spines. From it one or several arms may extend outward and upward. Late in the spring corollas of flowers with white petals and yellow hearts appear on the tips of trunk and arms. A fruit then forms, containing juicy crimson pulp and thousands of small black seeds. For centuries the Papagos, who now prefer to be known by their own name, Tohono O'odham, have made summer trips to temporary camps in nearby stands of saguaro to harvest the fruit. The

Are they beautiful these plants and shrubs of the desert? ... If (by beautiful) you mean something appropriate to its setting ..., then the desert will show forth much that people nowadays are beginning to think beautiful.

SAGUARO TRUNKS, AJO MOUNTAINS,
ORGAN PIPE CACTUS NATIONAL MONUMENT, ARIZONA.

pulpy flesh is eaten fresh or cooked, the seeds are ground into flour, and the juice is made into wine for an annual rain ceremony.

Dry years retard the saguaro's growth, while a wet season swells its vertical flutes or pleats. Saguaro skyscrapers, like our own, house many tenants. Hawks nest in the junctions of trunks and arms. In its pithy column, small round holes like window openings reveal where woodpeckers have dug in to nest and where sometimes tiny elf owls and other birds have taken up residence. Wood rats and ants burrow into its base.

The creosote bush or greasewood *(Larrea tridentata)* almost rivals the sagebrush's wide coverage, growing everywhere throughout the Sonoran Desert. It is a gray-green bush about five feet high, with small leaves and tiny yellow flowers which appear each spring. One of the most hardy plants with deep roots, it can endure years without rain.

Only a thick handbook can catalog the amazing number of plants, shrubs, cacti, and trees that have adapted to life in the desert. All have the same family talents for protecting themselves from the fierce rays of the sun and conserving water.

Animals have adapted to the desert range from bighorn sheep and wild burros down through coyotes, bobcats, peccaries or javelinas, and the coatimundi of northern Mexico, to tiny mice, lizards, rattlesnakes, and Gila monsters. And there are birds in varieties almost too numerous to mention. In Death Valley, for example, have been found 200 species of birds, 80 animals, 50 reptiles, and 1,000 plants. Reported in the Big Bend National Park are 382 species of birds, 75 of mammals, and 55 of reptiles including a copperhead snake found only there. How fruitful and prolific is our Mother Earth even in the hot and arid desert.

One other species of life-forms has adapted in its own ways to life in the North American Desert—humankind.

For a minimum of 12,000 years, the desert has been sparsely occupied by comparatively small groups of prehistoric people. They have left records of their life in stone tools, arrowheads, petroglyphs or rock writing, potsherds, and the ruins of cliff dwellings and surface pueblos.

Outstanding among the early inhabitants were the Hohokam people who developed a distinctive culture along the Gila River, centering near Casa Grande, Arizona. Who the first Hohokam arrivals were is not known. It is conjectured they might have wandered here from Mexico as primitive nomads about the time of Christ, living in pit houses and existing on wild foods. By A.D. 600 they had begun to develop a culture showing a Mexican influence. They constructed ditches and canals to carry water from the Gila to irrigate their fields of corn, squash, and cotton; one of these networks covered more than 150 miles. Settled into a sedentary life, the Hohokam during the following centuries experienced the highest or "classical" phase of their culture. They built a ceremonial ball court 200 feet long and truncated earthen pyramids, both similar to those anciently used throughout Mesoamerica. Also they fired excellent pottery and fashioned ornaments from shells brought in trade from the Gulf of California.

About A.D. 1350 their culture began to decline; villages were abandoned, and the people dispersed. Some authorities believe most of the Hohokam people migrated back to Mexico or elsewhere, leaving the area to a slow influx of members of other neighboring cultures—Anasazi, Mogollon, the

Yuman tribes of Quechans, Cocopas, Mohaves, and Maricopas. Others believe their descendants are the Pimas and Tohono O'odham.

In any case, the Hohokam had established the longest lasting, tribal society in the North American Desert, and had made the first major attempt to reclaim part of the desert with their network of canals. Why it did not further develop into one of the first and still enduring indigenous civilizations, like those of the Hopis and Navajos on the higher Colorado Plateau, might be attributed to the desert's eventual assertion of its own inviolability against reclamation.

It appears, then, that these elements of water, air, sunfire, and earth have largely modelled the physical shape and texture of the desert. Here, perhaps more than in other areas on the surface of our world, they seem to have attained a visible equilibrium. To these balanced forces all the desert's living forms have adapted in special ways, setting the desert apart from our larger, and more familiar, green world. Moreover, something about it, whatever it is, draws us to it. Is it the desert's vast emptiness, its harsh and arid unreality, its momentary moods and eternal mystery? Could it be that we have an unconscious affinity with the desert because the same creative four elements structure us both?

Such extravagant questions are prompted as we prepare for sleep upon the flat roof of an adobe house in the Sonoran Desert, gazing up at the silent stars which give us no answers. But one concept from the other side of the world offers a direction for our midnight speculations.

Buddhist religious philosophy asserts, like many other beliefs throughout the world, that man is a derivative summation of the four primal elements. From the fire element he derives his life heat. From the air element his breath of life. From the water element his life stream, his blood. From the earth element the solid substance of his body. And because he is more than a stationary organism, he derives

from them sentient qualities. With air he receives the facility of movement. With earth the sensitivity of touch. With water, consciousness. And with fire an aggregate of emotions. But man has a psychical as well as a physical nature. So Buddhist belief further asserts that the four elements endow him with equivalent passions. Fire and feelings give him attachment and lust. Air and volition the passion of envy. Water and consciousness his anger. And earth and the sense of touch his egoism.

This metaphysical concept of Eastern thought may not be readily acceptable to Western minds, but it perhaps deserves a closer look in light of modern man's ever-increasing interference with the working of the four elements.

Worldwide, we are contaminating all the waters, streams, rivers, lakes, and oceans. The air is being polluted by toxic fumes from industrial plants and automobiles. The earth is being destroyed by strip-mining, leveling of rain forests, soil erosion, and burial of toxic wastes. And with the weakening of the protective ozone shield, we are exposing ourselves to the sun's dangerous ultraviolet rays.

The North American Desert, like all the other deserts in the world, long was unchanged by mankind. For 10,000 years or more it had been sparsely occupied by small tribal groups, primitive but adaptive, who have left records of their life in stone tools, rock art, pottery, cliff-dwellings and surface pueblos, and miles of irrigation canals.

Only recently has our breed of intrusive Yankees adapted to life in the desert with broad cement highways; cities spreading out in immense urban sprawls; homes and high-rise condominiums with air conditioning systems; lawns and flower gardens and ever present swimming pools; dammed rivers forming immense lakes; and networks of irrigation works projected eventually to water the entire desert. It seems, offhand, that we late desert dwellers are not

How long ago did that aboriginal band come trailing over these trackless deserts to find and make a home in a barren mountain standing on a bed of sand?

PREHISTORIC ROCK ART, GILA RIVER VALLEY, ARIZONA.

so much adapting to the desert as trying to adapt the desert to our way of life.

I don't believe that the projected conquest of the arid one-seventh of the world's surface can change its eternal character by technological sculpturing. I can't imagine the great Sahara turned into a vast green garden of fruits and veg etables. Something beyond the control of our technology is likely to interfere.

For if the Buddhist belief is sound, the four elements act psychically upon us as well as physically upon our outer world. Interconnected as are our inner and outer worlds in one universal body of creation, we are distorting our own lives by interfering with the natural action of these creative powers.

It is encouraging that many areas in the desert have been preserved as national parks and monuments. Yet attrition continues: off-road vehicles uproot the ground, destroy plantlife, disturb animals, and churn up clouds of dust. Hunters are decimating birds and animals. And thousands of deep wells are drawing water from underground faster than it is being replenished.

Despite these inroads upon the desert, its greater body remains untouched. To it millions of us make pilgrimages. We glimpse its brief display of spring flowers, find a breathing space free from urban smog, and, when confused and fragmented at heart, seek escape from our conscious mind.

In silence and solitude we find a spiritual oasis amidst the clamor of the world's voices and the tyranny of our unceasing conscious thoughts. How strangely familiar is this unfamiliar domain which mysteriously mirrors our unconscious. It calls forth instant response from that hidden font within us, eternal as the desert itself. □

—*Frank Waters*

Frank Waters has been writing about the American Southwest for more than 50 years, producing more than 20 books of fiction, biography, anthropology, ethnology, Indian myth and religion, history, and philosophy.

NORTH AMERICAN DESERTS

LEGEND

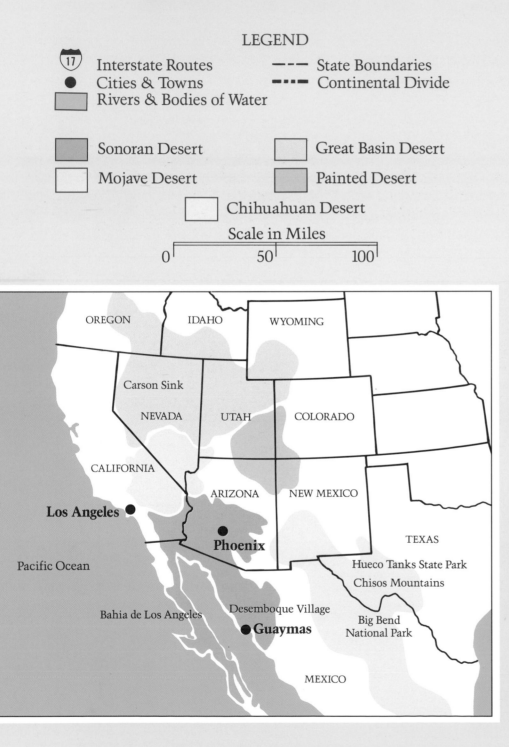

- **17** Interstate Routes
- ● Cities & Towns
- ▬ Rivers & Bodies of Water

- - - - State Boundaries
- - ·- Continental Divide

- Sonoran Desert
- Mojave Desert
- Great Basin Desert
- Painted Desert
- Chihuahuan Desert

Scale in Miles

0   50   100

OREGON   IDAHO   WYOMING

Carson Sink

NEVADA   UTAH   COLORADO

CALIFORNIA

ARIZONA   NEW MEXICO

Los Angeles ●

Phoenix ●

TEXAS

Hueco Tanks State Park

Chisos Mountains

Pacific Ocean

Desemboque Village

Bahia de Los Angeles   ● **Guaymas**

Big Bend National Park

MEXICO

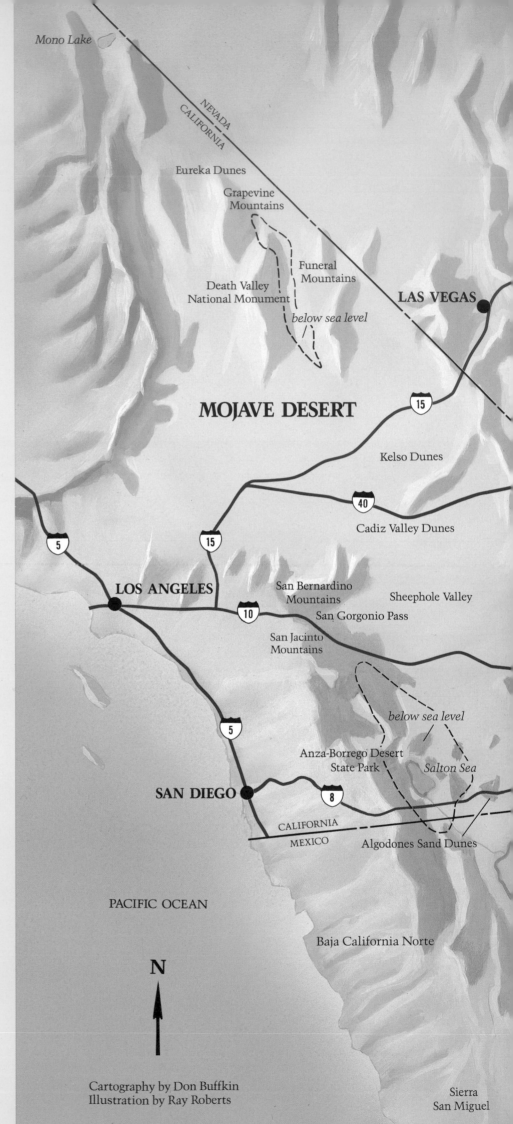

Mono Lake

NEVADA
CALIFORNIA

Eureka Dunes

Grapevine Mountains

Funeral Mountains

Death Valley National Monument

below sea level

LAS VEGAS ●

MOJAVE DESERT

15

Kelso Dunes

40

Cadiz Valley Dunes

5

LOS ANGELES ●

15

San Bernardino Mountains

Sheephole Valley

10

San Gorgonio Pass

San Jacinto Mountains

below sea level

5

Anza-Borrego Desert State Park

Salton Sea

SAN DIEGO ●

8

CALIFORNIA
MEXICO

Algodones Sand Dunes

PACIFIC OCEAN

Baja California Norte

N

Cartography by Don Buffkin
Illustration by Ray Roberts

Sierra San Miguel

GREAT BASIN DESERT

15

NEVADA
UTAH

Zion
National Park
Glen Canyon
National Recreation Area
● Kanab *Lake Powell*
Rainbow Bridge
National Monument

UTAH
COLORADO

ARIZONA
NEW MEXICO

Virgin
Mountains
Paiute Wilderness

Vermilion Cliffs
Paria Canyon
Wilderness
Antelope Canyon
Monument Valley

Navajo
National Monument

Shiprock

Navajo Reservoir

Virgin
River

Colorado

River

Chinle Wash

Navajo
Indian Reservation

Chaco Canyon
National Monument

ke Mead
Grand Wash Cliffs
ke Mohave

Canyon de Chelly
National Monument

SANTA FE

Grand Canyon
National Park

Hopi
Indian Reservation

Little

Colorado

PAINTED DESERT

40

ALBUQUERQUE

Wupatki
National Monument
San Francisco Peaks

Colorado

River

Petrified Forest
National Park

40

FLAGSTAFF

Red Rock—Secret
Mountain
Wilderness
Oak Creek Canyon

MOGOLLON RIM

ARIZONA
NEW MEXICO

Continental

Divide

25

Lake Havasu

Bill Williams River

Verde River

17

Sierra Anchas
Mazatzal
Mountains
Roosevelt Lake

Cibecue Creek
White
Mountains
Fort Apache

Rio Grande

CALIFORNIA
ARIZONA

Colorado

River

Salt River

10

PHOENIX

Tonto
National Monument

SONORAN DESERT

Eagle Tail
Mountains

10

Superstition
Mountains

San Carlos Lake

Gila

River

Elephant Butte Reservoir

Kofa
Mountains
Martinez Lake

Gila River

8

Santa

San Pedro

Galiuro
Mountains

Tularosa Valley

White Sands
National
Monument

YUMA
ma Desert
Tinajas Altas Mountains
Lechuguilla Desert
mino del Diablo "Devil's Highway"
Tule Mountains
Cabeza Prieta

Cruz

River

Picacho Peak

10

Santa Catalina
Mountains

River

LAS CRUCES

10

Tohono O'Odham
Indian Reservation

Ajo
Mountains
Coyote Mountains

Saguaro National
Monument

EL PASO

Gran Desierto

Organ Pipe Cactus
● National Monument
Lukeville

TUCSON

Chiricahua
Mountains

NEW MEXICO
MEXICO

TEXAS
MEXICO

Sierra del Pinacate

ARIZONA
MEXICO

19

Santa Rita
Mountains
Miller Peak
Huachuca
Mountains

SEA OF CORTEZ

NOGALES

CHIHUAHUAN DESERT

SONORAN DESERT

A Desert Journey

The late anthropologist, author, philosopher Loren Eisley asked "What is it we are a part of that we do not see?" For me, that question helps explain the meaning of the desert. I have experienced and related to the benign, empty desert. Its open spaces speak to me. In it I find time and room for intuition and insight to its beauty, and a sense of connectedness that delights and rewards me immensely.

The desert is a paradox. It is at once an experience of nurturing and discomfort, mystery and comprehension. The sounds of wind, earth, and sky fill my ears, but it is the powerful *silence* of the desert that tugs at my unconscious, inspires my imagination, until both the abstract and the real are perceived.

The sound, smell, clarity of air, and quality of light on the desert all invite my return. The many trips to the desert, while making the photographs for this book, combined to become one journey—a living experience of questions and answers, of exploration and discovery. Verbalizing this is difficult, as photographs are my language for communicating the mystery of this land form. These photographs are reference points along a journey that visualize the power and beauty of the desert.

The desert as subject includes such favorites as red rock country, cacti of the Sonoran Desert, sage-creosote expanses of the Mohave, bony ridges of granite and volcanics in the Yuman Desert and Cabeza Prieta, Big Bend National Park, and countless pictograph and petroglyph sites communicating messages from ancient peoples. The sand and silence of the Gran Desierto and Pinacate in Sonora, Mexico, the slot canyons with impassable choke rocks, the pools of precious water reflecting the sun as they evaporate, and the night sky become unique in their simplicity.

Dawn and evening light display subtleties of color and tone the most, and at those times, a deepened working motivation is most intense.

Seasonal changes are surprising, unpredictable, and

sometimes nonexistent. The most compelling lie between spring and summer, and between fall and winter. At times I have seen plants that reflect all four seasons in progression after a single rain shower.

The awakening of spring with an ephemeral blossoming of wildflowers can transform a tawny landscape of rock and sand into a carpet of color. On cue, life pops out of hibernation, then recedes back into the land continuing its natural cycle. Observing Nature's design and pattern, light and form, matched with a creative timing make up the recipe for unique moments of expression I have been open to.

I feel an empathy, that I am a part of this nature that is ever changing and never static—moving with a rhythmic harmony. Photographic expressions, the visual images, can transform the ego into a heightened sense of introspection and sensitivity, and bring a better understanding of our relationship to the scheme of things—for me, a sense of place.

I hope these photographs bring renewed sensitivity and realization of our desert biosphere. With its limitations, the land, and the two-mile-high layer of air above it, contain both the miracles of natural creation and the pollutions of civilization. We hold in our hands the potential for control by ingenuity or increasing loss by greed and overdevelopment of these fragile lands. Areas of superb beauty must be protected and preserved intact, for they belong to the people of the world, and not to the few who would use them for personal gain.

May this book help remind us that a pristine natural order does exist, and, with sensitive stewardship by us all, will continue to endure.

—*David Muench*

David Muench strives to record the spirit of the land in his photography. His more than 20 books and numerous one-man exhibits display images of the natural world from North America and Hawaii.

CREATION FIRE

Even here in the desert where (the sunlight) falls fierce and hot as a rain of meteors, it is the one supreme beauty to which all things pay allegiance.

(LEFT) RIDGELINES,
GRAND CANYON NATIONAL PARK, ARIZONA.
(ABOVE) DESERT PAVEMENT, SIERRA DEL PINACATE,
PINACATE PROTECTED ZONE, SONORA, MEXICO.

Fire has been at work here as well as wind and
water. The whole country has a burnt and
scorched look proceeding from something more
fiery than sunlight.

(ABOVE) DESERT RIDGES, MILLER PEAK TOPROCK,
MILLER PEAK WILDERNESS, ARIZONA.
(OPPOSITE) VOLCANIC PAVEMENT AND PICACHO PEAK,
YUMAN DESERT, CALIFORNIA.

Tradition told that the Evil Spirit dwelt there,
and it was his hot breath that came up
every morning on the wind.
...Fire! He dwelt in fire!

(ABOVE) DUSK AT SHIPROCK, NEW MEXICO.
(OPPOSITE) OCOTILLO ON THE RIM
OF MACDOUGAL CRATER,
PINACATE PROTECTED ZONE,
SONORA, MEXICO.

YIELDING STONE

Tones of color, shades of light, drifts of air.... These are the most sensuous qualities in nature and in art.

(LEFT) DESERT WALL
IN THE SIERRA ANCHA MOUNTAINS, ARIZONA.
(ABOVE) SUNSET IN A SLOT CANYON,
SIERRA ANCHAS.

The edge of the wind
is always against
the stone.

SUPERSTITION MOUNTAINS,
SUPERSTITION WILDERNESS,
ARIZONA.

(FOLLOWING) IRON-STAINED CROSSBEDDING
IN AN ERODED DUNE
IN NAVAJO SANDSTONE,
VERMILION CLIFFS-
PARIA CANYON WILDERNESS,
ARIZONA-UTAH.

The change from ... shore to table-land and
mountain no doubt took place very slowly.
Just how many centuries ago who may say?
Geologists may guess and laymen may doubt,
but the Keeper of the Seals
says nothing.

SOUTH RIM,
GRAND CANYON NATIONAL PARK,
ARIZONA.

Nothing human is of long
duration. Men and their deeds
are obliterated, the race itself
fades; but Nature goes calmly
on with her projects. She works
not for man's enjoyment but
for her own satisfaction....

(LEFT) RAINBOW BRIDGE NATIONAL MONUMENT, UTAH.
(ABOVE) WALL DESIGN IN NAVAJO SANDSTONE,
ZION NATIONAL PARK, UTAH.

The desert is overwhelmingly silent.... But you
look...down at the wash-outs and piled bowlders,
you look about at the wind-tossed, half-starved bushes;
and, for all the silence, you know
that there is a struggle for life, a war for place,
going on day by day.

(OPPOSITE) LICHEN ON NAVAJO SANDSTONE, ZION NATIONAL PARK, UTAH.
(ABOVE) DAWN. VERMILION CLIFFS-PARIA CANYON
WILDERNESS, ARIZONA-UTAH.

Therefore there is
silence — something
of the hush of the
deserts and the river
that flows between.

JUNCTION OVERLOOK,
CANYON DE CHELLY NATIONAL MONUMENT,
ARIZONA.

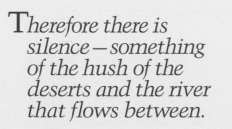

There are lonesome looking mountains lying off there by themselves on the plain, so still, so barren, so blazing hot under the sun.

SUNRISE AT THE MITTENS,
MONUMENT VALLEY NAVAJO TRIBAL PARK, ARIZONA-UTAH.

*T*he colors have undergone
years of "toning down" until
they blend and run together
like the faded tints of an
Eastern rug.

(BELOW) MOONRISE OVER
TOTEM POLE ROCK,
MONUMENT VALLEY NAVAJO
TRIBAL PARK, ARIZONA-UTAH.
(RIGHT) SANDSTONE FORMS,
COMB RIDGE, UTAH.

And for the deception of the eyes
    there is no wizard's cell
    nor magician's cabinet
    so admirably fitted for jugglery
    as this bare desert under sunlight.

ARTIST'S PALETTE, DEATH VALLEY NATIONAL MONUMENT, CALIFORNIA.

The weird solitude, the great
silence, the grim desolation,
are the very things with which every
desert wanderer eventually falls in love.

(ABOVE) VOLCANIC REMNANTS
ON A BAJADA IN THE SONORAN DESERT,
CABEZA PRIETA NATIONAL
WILDLIFE REFUGE, ARIZONA.
(RIGHT) MOUNT BANGS TOPROCK, VIRGIN MOUNTAINS,
PAIUTE WILDERNESS, ARIZONA.

(FOLLOWING, LEFT) KANAB "WONDERSTONE," KANAB, UTAH.
(FOLLOWING, RIGHT) PAINTED DESERT, ARIZONA.

The desert sand is finer than snow, and its curves and arches, as it builds its succession of drifts out and over an arroyo, are as graceful as the lines of running water.

(LEFT) SUNRISE OVER KELSO DUNES,
MOJAVE DESERT, CALIFORNIA.
(BELOW) WIND-BLOWN DUNE GRASS, KELSO DUNES,
MOJAVE DESERT, CALIFORNIA.

(FOLLOWING) DUNE CASCADE,
YEI BICHEI ROCKS,
MONUMENT VALLEY NAVAJO TRIBAL PARK, ARIZONA-UTAH.

FLOWING WIND

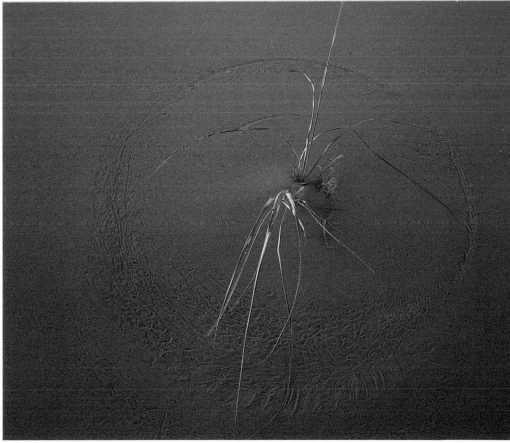

You *are always riding into the unexpected in these barren countries, stumbling upon strange phenomena, seeing strange sights.*

(ABOVE) KELSO DUNES, MOJAVE DESERT, CALIFORNIA.
(OPPOSITE) DUNAL CROSSBEDDING IN NAVAJO SANDSTONE,
VERMILION CLIFFS-PARIA CANYON WILDERNESS, ARIZONA-UTAH.

Nature never designed more fascinating country.... And everyone rides here with the feeling that he is the first one that ever broke into this unknown land, that he is the original discoverer.

(LEFT) INNER SLICKROCK,
ANTELOPE CANYON, ARIZONA.
(ABOVE) DRY SCULPTURE IN NAVAJO SANDSTONE,
GLEN CANYON NATIONAL RECREATION AREA, ARIZONA-UTAH.

71

N*ature never intended that we should fully understand. ... And shall we ever cease to wonder?*

(RIGHT) SANDSTONE FORMATIONS, VALLEY OF FIRE STATE PARK, NEVADA. (OPPOSITE) GRANITE CAVE IN THE TULE MOUNTAINS, CABEZA PRIETA NATIONAL WILDLIFE REFUGE, ARIZONA.

(FOLLOWING) MESA ARCH, CANYON-LANDS NATIONAL PARK, UTAH.

After the clash and roar of the
conflict in the canyons, how
impressive seems the stillness
of the desert, how appalling
the unbroken silence
of the lower river. Day after day
it moves southward, but
without a sound.

(LEFT) SUNSET AT CANYON DE CHELLY
NATIONAL MONUMENT, ARIZONA.
(BELOW) RAINSTORM IN THE SIERRA ANCHAS, ARIZONA.

PRECIOUS WATER

It is quite another country
when you come to examine it piece by piece.

(ABOVE) STORM CLEARING, MONUMENT VALLEY NAVAJO TRIBAL PARK, ARIZONA-UTAH.
(OPPOSITE) BUCKSKIN CANYON IN THE
VERMILION CLIFFS-PARIA CANYON WILDERNESS,
ARIZONA-UTAH.

(FOLLOWING) A CLOUD-SHROUDED RIM
ON THE HIGH DESERT
IN OAK CREEK CANYON, ARIZONA.

What a wilderness of fateful buffetings! All the elemental forces seem to have turned against it at different times.

(LEFT) A SMALL SANDSTONE BRIDGE
IN A NAVAJO SANDSTONE CANYON,
GLEN CANYON NATIONAL RECREATION AREA,
ARIZONA-UTAH.
(BELOW) SALT PODS IN A POOL AT BADWATER,
DEATH VALLEY NATIONAL MONUMENT, CALIFORNIA.

The cloud-bursts are
rushing down the
mountain's side and
through the torn
arroyos as though
they would wash the
earth into the sea.

VIRGIN RIVER CANYON,
VIRGIN MOUNTAINS,
PAIUTE WILDERNESS, ARIZONA.

(FOLLOWING LEFT) SANDSTONE SLOT
POOL IN NAVAJO CANYON, GLEN
CANYON NATIONAL RECREATION
AREA, ARIZONA-UTAH.
(FOLLOWING RIGHT) PADRE BAY AND
GUNSIGHT BUTTE AT DUSK, LAKE
POWELL, ARIZONA-UTAH.

The bed of the stream seems
to have sunken down,
but in reality it is rising
in steps and falls
ever increasing in size.
The stream itself has grown
much larger, swifter,
more noisy.

(LEFT) CASCADE ON CIBECUE CREEK,
FORT APACHE INDIAN RESERVATION,
ARIZONA.
(OPPOSITE) TOROWEAP,
GRAND CANYON NATIONAL PARK, ARIZONA.

It may be thought odd that the river
should change so radically from the clear
blue-green of its fountain-head
to the opaque red of its desert stream.

(ABOVE) GENTLE CASCADE IN BEAR CANYON,
SANTA CATALINA MOUNTAINS, ARIZONA.
(RIGHT) HAVASU FALLS, HAVASUPAI INDIAN RESERVATION, ARIZONA.
(MARC MUENCH PHOTO)

(FOLLOWING) COLORADO CANYON
OF THE RIO GRANDE, TEXAS — CHIHUAHUA, MEXICO.

The oases are strange because bright green foliage and moisture of any kind seem out of place on the desert.... Yet at times it is a land of heavy cloud-bursts and wash-outs.

(LEFT) DAWN AT QUITOBAQUITO, ORGAN PIPE CACTUS NATIONAL MONUMENT, ARIZONA.
(BELOW) DESERT STORM, SANTA CATALINA MOUNTAINS, ARIZONA.

THE LIVING SEED

*There is a war of elements
and a struggle for existence
going on here that for ferocity
is unparalleled elsewhere
in nature.*

(ABOVE) PRICKLY PEAR CACTUS,
SIERRA ANCHA WILDERNESS, ARIZONA.
(LEFT) HEDGEHOG CACTUS IN PAHOEHOE LAVA,
TULAROSA VALLEY, NEW MEXICO.

And wherever you go, by land or by sea, you
shall not forget that which you saw not but rather
felt — the desolation and the silence of the desert.

(BELOW) CARDON CACTI AT DAWN ON THE SHORES OF BAHIA DE
LOS ANGELES, BAJA CALIFORNIA NORTE, MEXICO.
(OPPOSITE) CLAY EROSION IN JASPER FOREST, PETRIFIED FOREST
NATIONAL PARK, ARIZONA.

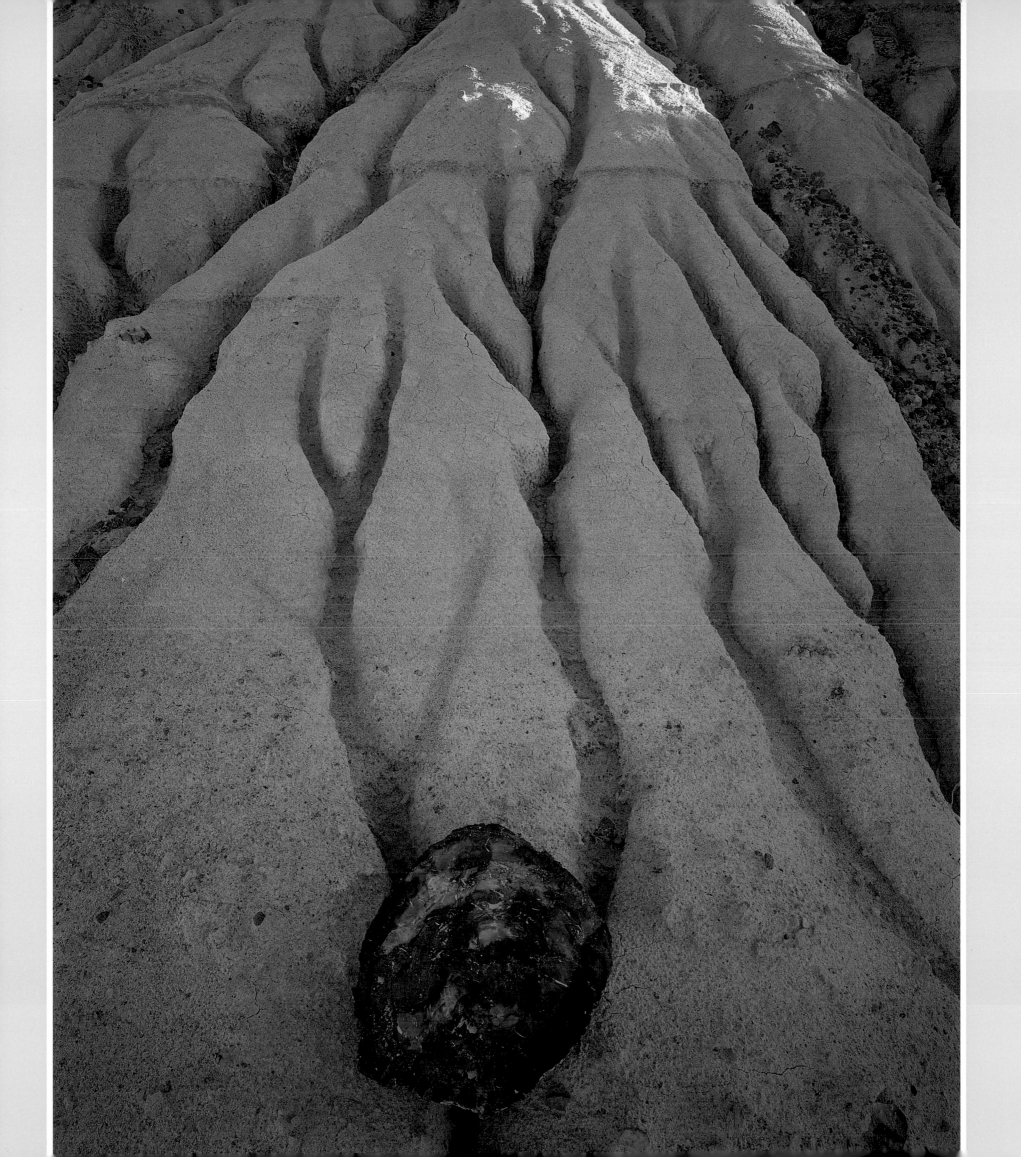

Mystery — *that haunting
sense of the unknown —
is all that remains.*

(LEFT) PEDESTAL LOGS, PETRIFIED FOREST NATIONAL
PARK, ARIZONA.
(ABOVE) LOG FRAGMENTS, JASPER FOREST, PETRIFIED
FOREST NATIONAL PARK, ARIZONA.

Strange growths of a strange land! ... And yet strange, perhaps, only to us who have never known their untrumpeted history.

(LEFT) SAGUARO CACTUS SKELETON, WEST UNIT OF SAGUARO
NATIONAL MONUMENT, ARIZONA.
(ABOVE) RICE GRASS AND RABBITBRUSH IN CANYONLANDS
NATIONAL PARK, UTAH.

(FOLLOWING, LEFT) ANCIENT BRISTLECONE PINE, TELESCOPE PEAK,
ABOVE PANAMINT VALLEY DUNES, DEATH VALLEY NATIONAL
MONUMENT, CALIFORNIA.
(FOLLOWING, RIGHT) DESERT RIDGES, GALIURO WILDERNESS, ARIZONA.

You will find every one of
(these plants) admirably fitted
to endure. They are marvelous
engines of resistance.

(BELOW) TEDDY BEAR CHOLLAS, BRITTLEBUSH, AND
ORGAN PIPE CACTUS IN ORGAN PIPE CACTUS
NATIONAL MONUMENT, ARIZONA.
(OPPOSITE) CLUSTERS OF HEDGEHOG CACTI, A
PRICKLY PEAR, AND AGAVES IN THE MAZATZAL
WILDERNESS, ARIZONA.

The tall fluted column of the sahuaro, sometimes fifty feet high, is little more than an upright cistern for holding moisture.

SAGUARO CACTI IN THE
SUPERSTITION WILDERNESS, ARIZONA.

It is the broadest, the simplest,
and in many respects the
sublimest sunset imaginable—
a golden dream with
the sky enthroned in glory.

JOSHUA TREES NEAR
THE GRAND WASH CLIFFS,
ARIZONA.

*Nature's work is all of it good,
all of it purposeful, all of it
wonderful, all of it beautiful.*

MANZANITA DESIGN, MAZATZAL WILDERNESS, ARIZONA.

The most common clouds of all are the cumuli.… As the sun disappears below the line… they darken into lilac and purple.

(OPPOSITE) CLOUDS GATHER OVER YUCCA AND THE GALIURO
MOUNTAINS, ARIZONA.
(ABOVE) MOUNTAIN PALMS OASIS, ANZA-BORREGO DESERT STATE
PARK, CALIFORNIA.

(FOLLOWING, LEFT) CHOLLA AND BARREL CACTI AND FAN PALMS
AT CARRIZO PALMS, ANZA-BORREGO DESERT STATE PARK,
CALIFORNIA.
(FOLLOWING, RIGHT) BOOJUM AND CARDON, SIERRA SAN MIGUEL,
BAJA CALIFORNIA NORTE, MEXICO.

*All the cacti are brilliant
in the flowers they bear.*

PRICKLY PEAR CACTUS,
CHISOS MOUNTAINS,
BIG BEND NATIONAL PARK, TEXAS.

Not in the spots of earth where plenty breeds
indolence do we meet with the perfected type. It
is in the land of adversity, and out of much pain
and travail that finally emerges the highest
manifestation.

(ABOVE) A CANE CHOLLA IN BLOOM AND AN AGAVE, CHIRICAHUA
MOUNTAINS, ARIZONA.
(RIGHT) A BEAVERTAIL CACTUS BLOOMS AT SUNSET,
KOFA NATIONAL WILDLIFE REFUGE, ARIZONA.

*S*ometimes beds of these flowers extend for miles, spreading in variegated sweeps of color, apparently undulating like a brilliant carpet swayed by the wind.

(ABOVE) MEXICAN POPPIES AND LUPINE ON THE TOHONO
O'ODHAM INDIAN RESERVATION NEAR THE COYOTE MOUNTAINS,
ARIZONA.
(OPPOSITE) DUNE PRIMROSES IN SHEEPHOLE VALLEY ON THE
MOJAVE DESERT, CALIFORNIA.

(FOLLOWING, LEFT) BLOOMS OF HEDGEHOG CACTUS IN THE
LOWER SONORAN DESERT.
(FOLLOWING, RIGHT) A BARREL CACTUS AND AN ELEPHANT TREE,
DESEMBOQUE, SONORA, MEXICO.

TRACINGS OF ANCIENT MAN

*But what brought them to seek
a dwelling place in the desert?*

(LEFT) WHITE HOUSE,
AN ANASAZI RUIN IN
CANYON DE CHELLY NATIONAL
MONUMENT, ARIZONA.
(ABOVE) A SALADO RUIN
IN THE SIERRA ANCHA
WILDERNESS, ARIZONA.

*Was it that they loved the open country,
the hot sun, the treeless wastes,
the great stretches of mesa, plain, and valley?
Ah; that is more than likely.*

(ABOVE) CLIFF DWELLING AT ANGEL SPRINGS, SUPERSTITION
WILDERNESS, ARIZONA.
(OPPOSITE) KEET SEEL, ANASAZI RUINS IN NAVAJO NATIONAL
MONUMENT, ARIZONA.

Is that the way our globe shall perish? Who can say? Nature plans the life; she plans the death; it must be that she plans aright.

(LEFT) PALATKI RUIN,
RED ROCK-SECRET
MOUNTAIN WILDERNESS, ARIZONA.
(ABOVE) SALADO RUIN,
TONTO NATIONAL MONUMENT, ARIZONA.

(FOLLOWING) LOMAKI RUIN AND SAN FRANCISCO PEAKS,
WUPATKI NATIONAL MONUMENT, ARIZONA.

Here the scouts could see far away the thin
string of foemen winding snake-like over the
ridges of the desert, could see them grow in size
and count their numbers, could look down
upon them at the foot of the mountain
and yell back defiance
to the challenge coming up the steep sides.

(OPPOSITE) WALL OF AN ANASAZI RUIN IN CHINLE WASH, UTAH.
(BELOW) ANASAZI RUIN IN ZION NATIONAL PARK, UTAH.

They lived here, it may be from necessity at first, and then stayed on because they loved the open wind-blown country.

(LEFT) FIVE FACES PICTOGRAPH, CANYONLANDS NATIONAL PARK, UTAH.
(ABOVE) PICTOGRAPHS, HUECO TANKS STATE HISTORIC PARK, TEXAS.

When man is gone, the sand and heat will come back to the desert. The desolation of the kingdom will live again... serene in its solitude.

PICTOGRAPHS,
RED ROCK-SECRET MOUNTAIN WILDERNESS,
ARIZONA.

The deserts should never be
reclaimed. They are the
breathing-spaces of the west
and should be preserved forever.

PETROGLYPH IN THE WEST UNIT
OF SAGUARO NATIONAL MONUMENT,
ARIZONA.

The life of the desert lives only by virtue of adapting itself to conditions of the desert. Even man...must endure the same heat, thirst, and hunger or perish.

(OPPOSITE) NEWSPAPER ROCK, INDIAN CANYON, UTAH.
(ABOVE) PETROGLYPHS IN THE EAGLE TAIL MOUNTAINS, ARIZONA.

This stone wall stands as their
monument, but it tells no date
or tale of death.

(ABOVE) PETROGLYPH, GILA RIVER VALLEY, ARIZONA.
(RIGHT) PICTOGRAPH, ANZA-BORREGO DESERT
STATE PARK, CALIFORNIA.

ADVICE TO DESERT TRAVELERS

In 1922, after he had walked and ridden horseback in the desert, John Van Dyke described his experience:

"I wore a half-Indian, half-Mexican costume, consisting of nothing but a thin cotton shirt and trousers, a straw hat, and moccasins on my feet. I discarded impedimenta for both myself and my horse and travelled as lightly as possible. All the pots and pans and flasks and opera-glasses that generally make weight in a camping-kit were left behind. I carried a rifle, a small shovel, a hatchet, a pair of light blankets, a small pan and some tin cups for cooking, a gallon of water, and several sacks of condensed food. I made my own condensation by grinding to a powder parched corn, beans, coffee, chocolate, and dried venison. ... I had merely to pour a few tablespoonfuls of it into a cup, add water, stir with a stick, and drink. I could go for twelve hours on less than half a cupful of it.

"Besides this mixture I carried tablets of chocolate, closely packed dried figs, a few shelled almonds, a little bacon, some flour, salt, tea, and a small bottle of saccharine. I had with me a single-barrelled twenty-two caliber Chicopee pistol, with which I shot rabbits, desert quail, doves, and other small game. My whole outfit weighed perhaps less than fifty pounds."

Van Dyke also used his head when it came to water. He knew his horse was good for about 50 miles without water. So if he didn't know where the next source of water would be, and failed to find one after 20 miles, he would simply return to the water source at which he'd started and try another direction the next day. It helped, of course, that he had no particular destination in mind and was "riding the desert for the mere joy of exploring it, ... the fancy of a madman."

Today's desert traveler is far more likely to be riding a motor-driven wheeled vehicle than a horse, but even for those enjoying this modern luxury, there are some common sense rules to keep in mind. The first is to remember that deserts are, by definition, dry places. So carrying water is always a fine idea. A few gallons stowed in the vehicle for emergencies should handle average situations, remembering that both people and most cars need water. Canned drinks, including juices, make a good addition. Drinking water from lakes or streams should be avoided, but if you must consume it, boil it first.

It's always wise to carry good road maps whether you stay on the pavement or decide to drive off of it. If you use unpaved back roads, make local inquiry concerning their condition. Being confronted by washouts is always a possibility. So is getting stuck in sand, in which case you should

I*f we would know the great truths, we must seek them at the source.*

reduce the air pressure in your tires to 15 psi to provide better traction. This means you'll need a pump to reinflate them after you're out of the sand. Having a shovel along for back country travel is mandatory.

Hauling spare gasoline is often advisable; gasoline stations are few and far between in many areas of the desert. And never fill a spare gas can to the top.

You hardy souls bent on heading into really remote country should let others know where you plan to go and when you plan to return. If possible, travel tandem with people in another vehicle, carrying a tow chain just in case. Always carry a jack, tools for car maintenance, extra fan belts, and oil; make sure your battery is in good condition; and have one, or even two, spare tires. Hide an extra key outside the car should you go hiking in the wilderness. And it never hurts to have a warm sleeping bag along although you may not plan to spend a night out. Deserts, even in summer, can be chilly at night, and should you get stuck, a sleeping bag could come in handy.

Sleeping in arroyos or other seemingly dry drainageways is never advisable, but especially so during the summer rainy season. Monsoon-like rains send tremendous quantities of water roaring downstream, and unwary campers have been known to get soaked, and have even drowned, as a result of such flash floods generated by distant storms, some of them miles away. Moreover, one should never drive through an arroyo or drainageway in flood stage. Wait it out. The waters will soon recede.

For people who contemplate serious back country desert travel, doing a little reading in advance is advisable. There are several excellent and inexpensive books on the subject, including the *Arizona Highways* book *Outdoors in Arizona: A Guide to Hiking and Backpacking* (Phoenix, 1987), Adrienne Knute's *Away from the Crowd* (Irvine, California: Wide Horizons Press, 1981), Charles Lehman's *Desert Survival Handbook* (Phoenix: Primer Pubs, 1987), and Ernest E. Snyder's *Arizona Outdoor Guide* (Phoenix: Golden West Publishers, 1985).

Adding it all together, desert travel is far safer—and infinitely more rewarding and enjoyable—than travel on any of our cities' freeways. Indeed, many have gone to the desert for its curative powers. If one uses a little common sense, there is nothing in the desert to fear. For those few who are frightened in the face of these great open and unpopulated expanses, the fear is of nothingness itself.

—Bernard L. Fontana